MARVELOUS MACHINERY

RIDES AT WORK

By Nathan Lepora

**Consultant: Suzy Gazlay, M.A.,
science curriculum resource teacher**

Gareth Stevens
Publishing

Please visit our web site at www.garethstevens.com.
For a free catalog describing our list of high-quality books, call 1-800-542-2595 (USA)
or 1-800-387-3178 (Canada). Our fax: 1-877-542-2596

Library of Congress Cataloging-in-Publication Data
Lepora, Nathan.
      Marvelous Machinery: Rides at Work / Nathan Lepora.
        p. cm. – (Marvelous Machinery)
      Includes index.
      ISBN-10: 0-8368-8946-0   ISBN-13: 978-0-8368-8946-8 (lib. bdg.)
      ISBN-10: 0-8368-8951-7   ISBN-13: 978-0-8368-8951-2 (softcover)
      1. Rotational motion—Juvenile literature. 2. Force and
energy—Juvenile literature. I. Title.
      GV1860.R64L47 2008
      791.06'8—dc22   2007042116

This North American edition first published in 2008 by
Gareth Stevens Publishing
A Weekly Reader® Company
1 Reader's Digest Road
Pleasantville, NY 10570-7000 USA

This U.S. edition copyright © 2008 by Gareth Stevens, Inc. Original edition copyright © 2007 by ticktock
Media Ltd. First published in Great Britain in 2007 by ticktock Media Ltd., Unit 2, Orchard Business Centre,
North Farm Road, Tunbridge Wells, Kent, TN2 3XF United Kingdom

ticktock Project editor: Sophie Furse
ticktock Picture researcher: Lizzie Knowles
ticktock Project designers: Hayley Terry
With thanks to: Carol Ryback, Suzy Gazlay, and Justin Spain

Gareth Stevens Editor: Jayne Keedle
Gareth Stevens Creative Director: Lisa Donovan
Gareth Stevens Graphic Designer: Farimah Toosi

Picture credits (t=top; b=bottom; c=center; l=left; r=right):
Richard Bannister: 12-13, 17b, 19, 29. Cedar Point: 15, 28l. Imagebroker/Alamy: 1. Interactive Rides, Inc. USA:
11t. Joel Rogers/CoasterGallery.com: 16, 17t, 18. Shenval/Alamy: 20. Shutterstock: Cover, contents page, 4-5,
6-7 main and inset, 6t, 8-9, 21-23, 25t. Superstock: 24. John Taylor/Alamy: 10-11 main. Wikipedia: 28r.
www.coastersandmore.de: 26-27 main, 27 inset.

Printed in the United States of America

 2 3 4 5 6 7 8 9 10 09 08

CONTENTS

CHAPTER 1: MACHINES

How would you describe a roller coaster? You could mention the amazing speed, the dizzying heights, and the exciting twists and turns. Basically, though, a roller coaster is a machine.

WHAT IS A MACHINE?

A **machine** is a device that acts on another object. It might help you push or move something. People use machines to make a task easier. For example, a bicycle lets you move quickly with little effort. Other machines, such as roller coasters, are built just for fun! Machines can be as simple as a bottle opener or as complex as an airplane. Most have moving parts that work together to do a job.

THAT'S AMAZING!

Wheels and ramps are simple machines. Today, coaster cars roll along on wheels. The first roller coaster rides were sleds that ran down ramps of ice.

A loop-the-loop on a roller coaster. The wheels and track are parts of an exciting machine.

SIMPLE AND COMPLEX MACHINES

A simple machine has one of four basic components: **wheel**, **ramp**, **pulley**, and **lever**. All machines contain at least one of those things. A ramp is a very simple machine. It has no moving parts.

Complex machines often contain a number of smaller simple machines. For example, an engine may contain many moving parts that act as wheels and levers. Those simple machines work together to make the engine run.

Roller coasters are machines made of ramps and wheels.

Every hour, more than 1,000 people ride **Kumba**, at Superland in Israel.

DID YOU KNOW?

The world's first **tubular** steel roller coaster was the Matterhorn Bobsleds. It opened in 1959 at Disneyland in California. Walt Disney got the idea while visiting the Swiss Alps.

CHAPTER 2: WHEELS AND RAMPS

oller coasters use two basic types of simple machines – wheels and ramps. Wheels make the roller coaster cars move. The cars roll up and down ramps.

WHAT ARE WHEELS?

Our everyday lives depend upon the wheel. Without it, we would have no easy way to transport objects or ourselves. A wheel is a large circle that turns around an **axle** at its center. It is a simple machine.

Wheel turning on an axle

Rotational motion

Axle

WHAT ARE RAMPS?

A ramp is another simple and useful machine. We use ramps all the time without realizing it. A ramp is a slope, or **inclined plane.** Ramps have no moving parts. They make it easier for us to move objects from one height to another.

Pushing or pulling force

Ramp

A ramp shortens the distance over which an object must move. Lifting an object takes force. However, it takes less force to move an object along a ramp.

THE ROLLER COASTER MACHINE

Forces push and pull on an object to make it move or stop. **Gravity** and other forces power roller coasters. Gravity pulls all objects toward Earth. The force of gravity also makes objects speed up as they fall to the ground.

Gravity pulls this roller coaster down a slope. Its wheels allow a smooth ride at super-fast speeds.

CHAPTER 3: PULLEYS AND LEVERS

Pulleys and levers are two types of simple machines. Pulleys change the direction in which a force pulls. Levers use a **pivot** point to help move an object. A seesaw is a common example of a lever.

WHAT IS A PULLEY?

A wheel and rope make up a pulley. This simple machine is used to lift heavy objects. A rope loops around the wheel. An object can be attached to one end of the rope. Pulling down on the other end of the rope turns the wheel and lifts the object. Some roller coasters use pulleys to pull the cars up the first hill.

It takes less force to lift an object using a pulley.

A pulley in action

Rope

Wheel

Pulling force

Lifting force

THAT'S AMAZING!

X-scream in Las Vegas, Nevada, is a seesaw ride over the edge of the Stratosphere Tower!

X-scream riders rock on a giant teeter totter 866 feet (264 meters) in the air.

WHAT IS A LEVER?

A lever is a long bar that uses a pivot point. As one end is pushed down, the other end gets pushed up. The pivot point of a lever is not always in the middle. It can be at any point along the bar.

PIVOT IN THE CENTER OF LEVER

The weight of the two children pushes up the child at the other end.

PIVOT OFF-CENTER

With the pivot closer to the end of the bar, the weight of one child is enough to push up the two children.

CHAPTER 4: PROPULSION

There are two ways to get a roller coaster going. One way is to tow it to the top of a hill and let gravity pull it down. Another way is to **catapult** it into motion from a dead start.

GRAVITATIONAL PROPULSION

Gravity pulls everything toward the ground. It pulls heavier objects even faster. The force of gravity helps propel roller coaster cars. A **chain lift** pulls the cars to the top of the **lift hill**. This is the first and tallest hill on a roller coaster. Gravity and the **weight** of the cars pull them down and the fun begins!

ROLLER COASTERS AND AUTOMOBILES

Roller coaster cars and automobiles can both travel fast, but they are propelled in very different ways. Automobiles have engines that provide power. Roller coaster cars have no engine. They cannot move by themselves. A separate source of power is needed to start a roller coaster car.

The roller coaster car is pulled up the lift hill to the top.

Gravity propels the cars down the hill and through the ride.

THAT'S AMAZING!

Oblivion plunges riders 196 feet (60 meters) down an almost vertical drop at speeds up to 70 miles (110 kilometers) per hour.

LAUNCHED COASTERS

Some modern roller coasters are not pulled up a lift hill to be released. They are launched from the starting station, often shooting straight up a hill. These are called launched coasters.

MAGNETIC PROPULSION

One type of launch system uses magnetic propulsion. It works by using huge **electromagnets.** These produce a strong magnetic force when electricity passes through them. The magnets are fitted into the tracks and beneath the cars. Electricity changes the magnetic **poles** quickly to **attract** and **repel** the cars. That makes the cars **accelerate** around the tracks.

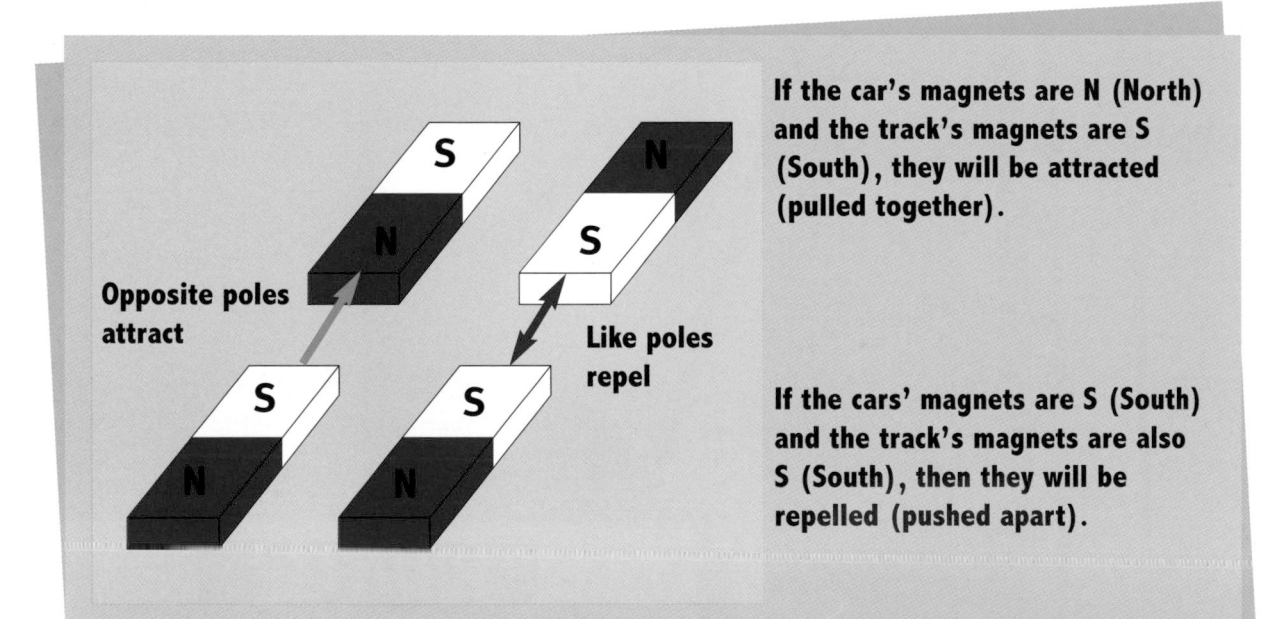

Opposite poles attract

Like poles repel

If the car's magnets are N (North) and the track's magnets are S (South), they will be attracted (pulled together).

If the cars' magnets are S (South) and the track's magnets are also S (South), then they will be repelled (pushed apart).

The launch starts with the **magnets** on the track changing their poles to those opposite the car's magnets. For example, the track is North and the cars are South. This attracts the cars forward. Then, once the cars reach that set of magnets, they change poles, repelling the cars toward the next set of magnets.

THAT'S AMAZING!

Wicked Twister in Sandusky, Ohio, uses as much electricity as a small town.

As the cars are repelled forward, the next set of magnets change their poles to attract the cars. That causes the cars to accelerate. This sequence continues until the train reaches its maximum speed.

Wicked Twister shoots 215 feet (65.5 m) into the air while twisting round and round.

CATAPULT LAUNCHES

Not all roller coaster rides begin with a slow ride up a hill. Some roller coasters launch the cars at high speeds. A catapult launch releases a huge burst of **energy** to propel the cars up the hill at great speed.

Dodonpa in Fujiyoshida, Japan, and Hypersonic XLC at Kings Dominion in Virginia both use **compressed air** to power their catapults.

WHAT IS COMPRESSED AIR?

When you blow up a balloon, you squeeze a lot of air into a tight space. The pressure, or force of the weight of that air, is greater than the pressure of air in the atmosphere. It is compressed air. If you untie the balloon, the force of the air escaping sends it flying. Compressed air does the same thing to a roller coaster car!

Hypersonic XLC uses sets of powerful magnets as brakes to stop the ride.

Compressed air is released behind the cars to launch them. The force of the air pushes them forward—and fast!

Riders accelerate with such force that their bodies feel four times heavier than normal!

On this section of Hypersonic XLC, the cars are weighed. The cars' weight is used to figure out how much air is needed. Heavier cars need a greater force to move them, so they need more air.

Dodonpa has the fastest launch of any coaster in the world. It catapults the cars to 107 miles (172 km) per hour in 1.8 seconds.

Roller coasters have frames made either of wood or steel. Each material provides a thrilling but unique ride. Wood and steel frames react differently as roller coaster cars roar over them.

WOODEN ROLLER COASTERS

Roller coaster builders have used wood frames for more than one hundred years. Wooden beams bolted together form a strong but flexible framework.

The wooden roller coaster Son of Beast in Ohio is made from 1.65 million feet (502,920 m) of wood and covers 12 acres (5 hectares).

PROPERTIES OF WOOD

Wood is a great material for roller coaster structures. It is lighter than steel but still quite strong. It flexes (bends) and sways slightly as the cars roll along. Wooden-framed roller coasters rattle and shake. Many roller coaster fans enjoy that feeling!

THAT'S AMAZING!

The world's oldest operating roller coaster is Leap-the-Dips in Lakemont Park, Pennsylvania. The wooden coaster opened in 1902.

Son of Beast in Ohio is the world's tallest wooden roller coaster. It is 218 feet (66 m) high.

STEEL ROLLER COASTERS

Many roller coaster frames are now built completely from steel. Their tracks are steel tubes joined to steel supports. Steel coasters offer a smoother ride than wooden coasters. Unlike wood, the steel frame does not move as the riders fly through incredible twists and loop-the-loops.

DID YOU KNOW?

A typical steel roller coaster like The Big One in Blackpool, UK, contains 2,481 tons (2,215 tonnes) of steel. Sixty thousand bolts hold it together.

From 1994 to 1996, **The Big One** was the world's fastest roller coaster, with top speeds of 86 miles (140 km) per hour. It lost its record to Fujiyama in Japan.

The use of steel in roller coasters allows for some amazing designs. Cars can loop-the-loop many times or twist around and around. Some rides even zoom along upside-down or have rotating seats.

The Incredible Hulk at Universal Studios' Islands of Adventure in Orlando, Florida

PROPERTIES OF STEEL

Steel is an ideal material for building roller coasters. It is very strong and can be molded into any shape. Long, curving sections are welded together to form **rigid** structures. That allows modern coasters to offer more sharp twists and turns than ever.

CHAPTER 6: STRONG STRUCTURES

The structure of a roller coaster is strong thanks to a series of vertical, horizontal, and crossbeam supports.

FANTASTIC FRAMEWORKS

Wooden roller coasters have an open framework of supports. Vertical (up-and-down) supports hold up the tracks. The structure is strengthened by horizontal supports and diagonal crossbeams.

SUPPORTING LOADS

Structures must withstand many forces without breaking. Most structures only need to support their own weight. Roller coaster frameworks must also stand up to additional forces as cars thunder around the tracks.

The framework of a wooden roller coaster

All structures need strong frames. The Eiffel Tower in Paris, France, has an open pattern of supporting beams. Its structure is similar to that of a roller coaster.

THAT'S AMAZING!

The Eiffel Tower contains more than 18,000 iron beams. It stands 1,063 feet (324 m) high and must support its own weight of 11,023 tons (10,000 tonnes). It was built in 1889.

THAT'S AMAZING!

Spaceship Earth at Disney's Epcot Center in Florida is a *geodesic dome.* It appears to be round but look closely and you'll see it is made up of many triangles—11,324 in all!

STRONG SHAPES

Look at a roller coaster's frame. You can see that the crossbeams and supports often form triangles. Engineers use the triangle design because it is a very strong shape. If you push downward or sideways on a triangle, it keeps its shape. That's because forces are spread out down its sides to the ground.

A force pushing on a square will usually squash it flat. A diagonal support or crossbeam strengthens a square shape by dividing it into triangles.

STEEL STRUCTURES

Like a triangle, a tube is another strong shape used in construction. Using metal tubes also helps reduce the weight of the material. Instead of solid steel pipes, a roller coaster frame is often made of hollow steel tubes.

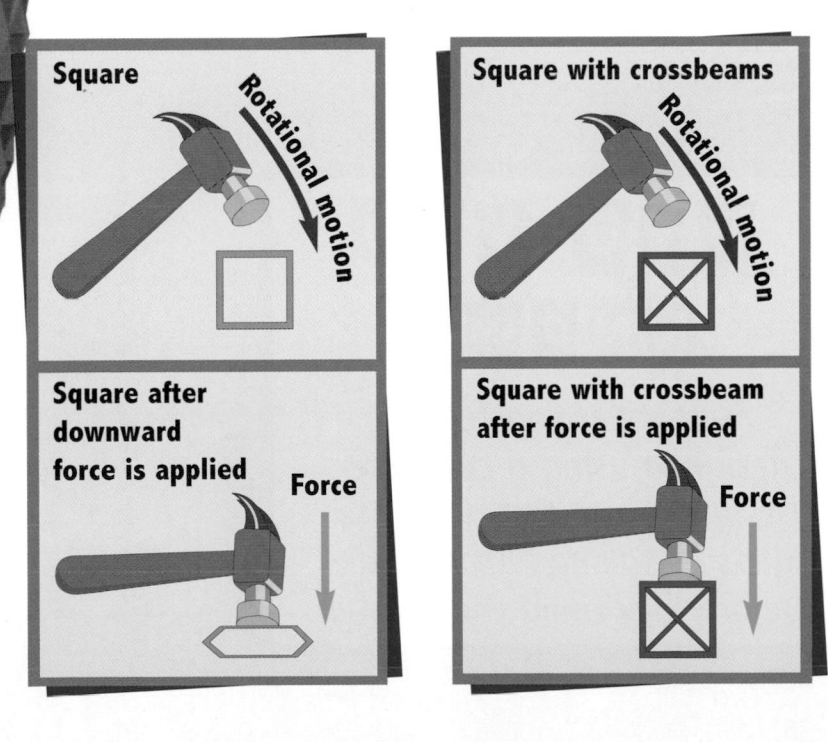

Square

Rotational motion

Square with crossbeams

Rotational motion

Square after downward force is applied

Force

Square with crossbeam after force is applied

Force

A triangle is a stronger shape than a square. Dividing a square into triangles helps it keep its shape when force is applied.

CHAPTER 7: DESIGN

Some roller coaster riders prefer smooth rides. Others seek out a jolting, edge-of-their seats experience. Engineers design roller coasters to give riders maximum thrills. Every roller coaster is different and will appeal to people in different ways.

The roller coaster **Typhoon** under construction in Lichtaart, Belgium

DID YOU KNOW?

Most roller coasters are designed using a computer. Designers can test drive their ideas by taking 'virtual rides' before they build the coaster.

DESIGNED TO THRILL

Designers must think about who will ride their machine. Roller coasters designed for small children should have gentle hills and slow cars. Thrill seekers (like you!) prefer dizzying heights, sharp turns, and incredible speeds.

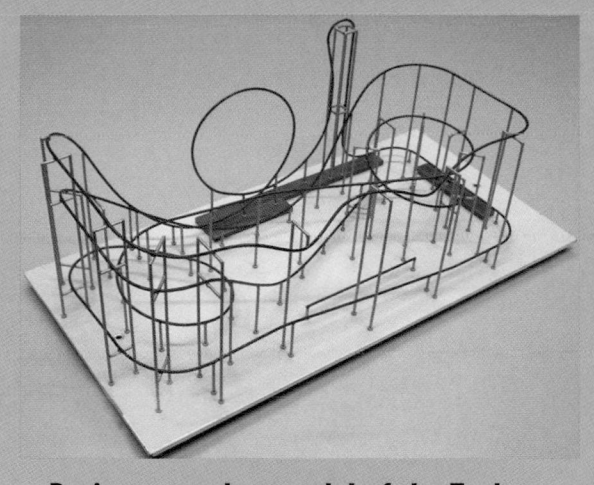

Designers made a model of the Typhoon before building began.

The designers know exactly how to make their rides more exciting. The first drop is usually the steepest and most terrifying. It catches riders by surprise. Low 'head chopper' bars are another scary design trick. They are positioned so it seems they just miss hitting riders' heads.

CHAPTER 8: NEW TECHNOLOGY

Future roller coasters could be taller than some skyscrapers. Others may have cars that use magnets to help them hover above the tracks. In Japan, high speed **Maglev** trains already do that!

HIGH-TECH ADVANCES

High-tech materials are likely to make future roller coasters even faster. For instance, the bodies of some cars are made from lightweight plastic **composites**. Composites are a mix of materials woven together. Plastic composites are very light and strong. Cars made from these materials weigh less, which allows them to travel faster.

Millennium Force at Cedar Point, Ohio, was the first roller coaster taller than 300 feet (91 meters).

FUTURE ROLLER COASTERS

Roller coaster fans welcome new developments. They make the rides faster and more exciting.

For instance, roller coasters keep getting taller. The tallest are called stratocoasters. Built in 2003, Top Thrill Dragster was the first such coaster. It's a towering 420 feet (128 m).

In 2005, Kingda Ka at Six Flags Great Adventure in New Jersey topped that. It's 456 feet (139 m) high. Heart-stopping drops and breathtaking speeds are what make roller coasters so thrilling!

The first stratocoaster, Top Thrill Dragster at Cedar Point, Ohio

DID YOU KNOW?

It takes Kingda Ka just 3.5 seconds to hit 128 miles (206 km) per hour. The roller coaster's biggest drop is a terrifying 418 feet (77 m).

GLOSSARY

Accelerate: to change in speed or direction; an object speeding up is said to accelerate

Attract: a force that pulls objects together

Axle: the central rod around which a wheel turns

Catapults: devices that launch objects at high speeds

Chain lift: a device used to tow a roller coaster up the first hill

Composite: made up of two or more other materials

Compressed air: air that is pressed into less space and held under high pressure. It is often used to power machines.

Electromagnet: a magnet that produces a powerful magnetic force when electricity flows through it

Energy: the ability to make something happen

Force: a push or pull on an object that can change the way it moves or behaves

Geodesic dome: a domelike structure made from polygons (many-sided shapes) joined together. Triangles are often used because they are such strong shapes.

Gravity: a force of attraction between objects; gravity pulls objects toward Earth

Inclined plane: a sloping ramp

Lever: a simple machine made from a bar on a pivot point. When one end of the bar is pushed down, the other end is pushed up.

Lift hill: the first and highest hill on a roller coaster

Machine: a device made up of moving parts that is used to do a job

Maglev trains: trains that use magnetic force to hover above the tracks

Magnets: metals that attract other metals (usually those that contain iron)

Pivot: a point around which an object turns

Poles: points where magnetic forces are strongest

Pulley: a simple machine made from a wheel and rope. It is used to lift objects.

Ramp: a simple machine that is a slope raised at one end. Ramps make it easier to move objects from one height to another.

Repel: to push away or apart

Rigid: stiff, unchanging in shape

Tubular: something made from tubes

Weight: the pull of gravity on an object's mass

Wheel: a round frame or object that turns on an axle to work machinery or move a vehicle

INDEX